D1443685

Southern **FOSSIL**
discoveries ● vol. 2

Giant
Predators
of the
Ancient
Seas

Judy Cutchins and Ginny Johnston

Pineapple Press, Inc. ● Sarasota, Florida

Inquiries should be addressed to:

Pineapple Press, Inc.
P.O. Box 3889
Sarasota, Florida 34230

www.pineapplepress.com

LIBRARY OF CONGRESS CATALOGING-IN-PUBLICATION DATA

Cutchins, Judy.
 Giant predators of the ancient seas / Judy Cutchins and Ginny Johnston.— 1st ed.
  p. cm. — (Southern fossil discoveries)
 Includes index.
  ISBN 1-56164-237-1 (alk. paper)
  1. Marine animals, Fossil—Juvenile literature. [1. Marine animals, Fossil. 2. Prehistoric animals.
3. Paleontology.] I. Johnston, Ginny. II. Title.

QE851 .C88 2001
566'.09162—dc21

                                                                                                2001021328

First Edition
10 9 8 7 6 5 4 3 2 1

Design by Carol Tornatore Creative Design

Printed in China

Contents

Art and Photo Credits

Acknowledgments

We wish to give very special acknowledgment to James P. Lamb, Ph.D., Department of Marine, Earth, and Atmospheric Sciences at North Carolina State University in Raleigh, North Carolina, and to Mark Uhen, Ph.D., Curator of Paleontology and Zoology at Cranbrook Institute of Science in Bloomfield Hills, Michigan. Their expertise and generosity have been invaluable in our work on *Giant Predators of the Ancient Seas*.

We gratefully acknowledge Mike Everhart, Oceans of Kansas Paleontology, for sharing his knowledge and his excellent photographs. We also thank David Dockery, Ph.D., and Michael Bograd, Mississippi Department of Environmental Quality, Jackson, Mississippi; Eleanor Daly, Ph.D., Curator of Paleontology, Mississippi Museum of Natural History, Jackson, Mississippi; Ed Hooks, Ph.D., Collections Manager, Alabama Museum of Natural History, Tuscaloosa, Alabama; Susan Henson, Collections Manager, McWane Center, Birmingham, Alabama; Neal Larson, Black Hills Institute of Geological Research, Hill City, South Dakota; Al Sanders, Ph.D., Curator of Natural Sciences, Charleston Museum, Charleston, South Carolina; James Westgate, Ph.D., Lamar University, Beaumont, Texas; James Knight, Ph.D., Curator of Paleontology, South Carolina State Museum, Columbia, South Carolina; and Judith A. Schiebout, Ph.D., LSU Museum of Natural History, Baton Rouge, Louisiana. We greatly appreciate the cooperation and assistance of these professionals.

One

Fossils from Ancient Seas

How do we know what kinds of giant predators swam in prehistoric seas? People find fossils of these extinct animals, and scientists use these clues to identify creatures that lived in the oceans long ago.

The sea bottom provided ideal conditions for fossil formation. Countless microscopic and larger shelled animals lived in the sea. When they died, their empty shells settled on the seafloor, building up over time as layers of sediment. Mud, clay, and sand were deposited in the sea by rivers. Larger animals that died in the water or were washed in from the shore were buried by the sediment. Some hard parts, such as teeth and bones, became fossils. Over time, sediment layers grew hundreds or even thousands of feet thick. The weight of top layers packed deeper layers into a sedimentary rock called limestone.

Forming Fossils

When the skeletons and shells of animals are buried for many years under the right conditions, certain minerals gradually replace the material in the bones, teeth, and shells. This is one way fossils are formed.

LIFE IN THE PAST
MYA = Million Years Ago

CENOZOIC ERA

RECENT
10,000 YA - Present

PLEISTOCENE
1.8 MYA - 10,000 YA

PLIOCENE
6 MYA - 1.8 MYA

MIOCENE
23 MYA - 6 MYA

OLIGOCENE
38 MYA - 23 MYA

EOCENE
54 MYA - 38 MYA

PALEOCENE
65 MYA - 54 MYA

MESOZOIC ERA

CRETACEOUS
141 MYA - 65 MYA

JURASSIC
195 MYA - 141 MYA

TRIASSIC
235 MYA - 195 MYA

Change has always been part of the earth's history. Mountains have been uplifted and climates have warmed and cooled. Sea level has been high at times and low at others. Over millions of years, huge numbers of species of plants and animals have lived and died out.

Parts of the southeastern United States that were covered with seawater in prehistoric times are today known as the southern Coastal Plain. This part of North America is now dry, sandy land. But it was underwater for millions of years when the earth's sea level was higher than it is today. When sea level is high, more land is underwater. When sea level falls, there is more dry land. Scientists search for fossils in the Coastal Plain to learn what kinds of animals inhabited the prehistoric sea.

After sea creatures die, their bodies settle to the bottom and are buried by sediment.

9

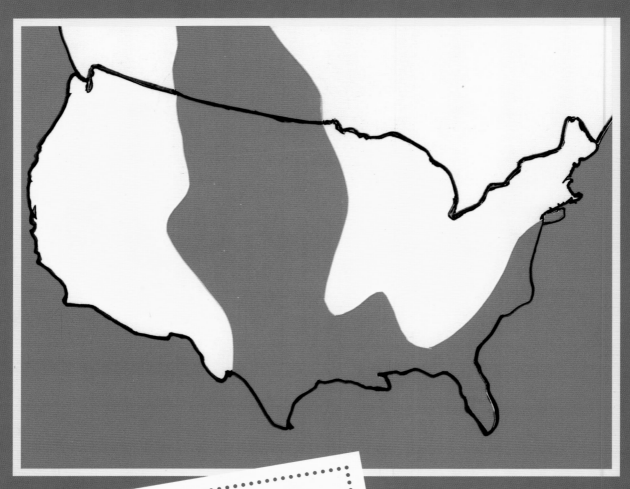

During the Cretaceous, sea level was so high that a shallow sea covered much of North America.

Finding Fossils

Limestone lies beneath the sand and soil of the southern Coastal Plain. Limestone is not as hard as most rock and is easily eroded by rain and rivers that flow over it. Fossils are usually harder than limestone and are exposed as the rock around them wears away.

Scientists search for fossils of sea predators in the areas that were once covered by seawater.

Fossil vertebrae can be seen as limestone erodes.

two

Monster Sea Lizards

Paleontologists search ancient limestone for fossils. They have found fossil proof of the most awesome sea predators that ever lived—seagoing lizards called mosasaurs. These giant reptiles swam in the Cretaceous seas while dinosaurs walked on land.

From thousands of fossil clues, scientists have identified different species of mosasaurs that lived during the Cretaceous. *Tylosaurus* was the biggest mosasaur in the warm sea of North America. This giant, over forty feet long, attacked anything that moved when it was hungry.

This 26-foot-long *Tylosaurus* skeleton discovered in the Midwest is on display at the Georgia Southern University Museum in Statesboro.

The Best Mosasaur Fossils

More Cretaceous limestone is exposed at the surface in the Midwestern states of Kansas and the Dakotas than in the South. Many nearly complete mosasaur skeletons have been discovered in those states. Most mosasaur fossils found in the South are teeth or fragments of skulls, jaws, backbones (vertebrae), and ribs. The skeletons from the Midwest are used to identify fossils found in the South.

A large Cretaceous sea turtle becomes prey as it is captured in the enormous jaws of a mosasaur.

Skulls, jaws, and teeth are some of the most important fossils that paleontologists find. One *Tylosaurus* skull discovered in Texas was almost six feet long. *Tylosaurus* had wide, cone-shaped teeth that curved slightly back toward the throat. A *Tylosaurus* could pierce shells and crush bony animals with its teeth and strong jaws. Like all mosasaurs, *Tylosaurus* had no chewing or grinding teeth. It would have swallowed prey whole or in large chunks. In the roof of the mouth were two rows of tiny teeth called pterygoids. Pterygoids helped a mosasaur work food down its throat.

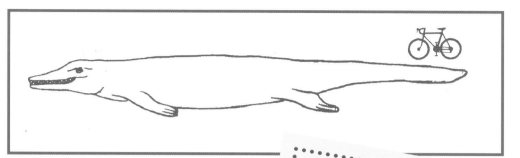

Under the summer sun, paleontologists from the University of Alabama dig out fossils of a giant mosasaur.

A few mosasaurs have been found along with the remains of their last meals. From this evidence, scientists know that *Tylosaurus* fed on bony fish, sharks, sea birds, mollusks, and smaller mosasaurs.

Scientists study fossil vertebrae, or backbones, to understand how a mosasaur swam. *Tylosaurus* was a powerful animal that could swim far and dive deep. Swinging its tail from side to side like an alligator, *Tylosaurus* could glide slowly through the water or dart after its prey with amazing quickness. It used front flippers to make fast turns.

Giant Lizards

The skeletons of mosasaurs are very much like those of monitor lizards, the largest lizards living today. Monitor lizards are carnivores that live in tropical countries. Some kinds of monitors are excellent swimmers that hunt in open water. Scientists study the behavior of monitor lizards to find clues about how mosasaurs may have lived. Observing living animals in their natural habitats helps researchers understand prehistoric life.

The carnivorous water monitor lizard of Southeast Asia can reach a length of 7 feet and is an excellent swimmer.

Hinged Jawbones

Each side of a mosasaur's lower jaw was hinged about halfway back. These joints and the muscles attached to them allowed the jawbones to flex as the mosasaur worked prey into its mouth and down its throat.

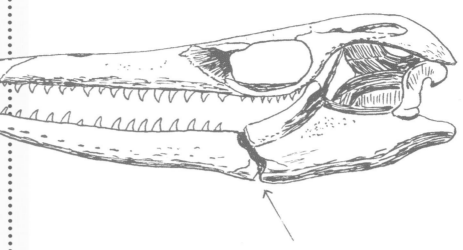

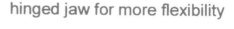

hinged jaw for more flexibility

Because these vertebrae are still together, they provide clues about how the mosasaur moved. "Swimming muscles" would have been attached to the flat piece of each vertebra. (The camera lens cover is for size comparison.)

Muscle Marks

Vertebrae provide many valuable clues for paleontologists. Marks on the vertebrae show where muscles were attached. The size of each mark is a clue to the size of the muscle. Large marks on tail vertebrae, for example, would be a clue that strong swimming muscles were once attached there.

Sometimes Predator, Sometimes Prey

Many kinds of ammonites grew as large as car tires and were excellent predators. They had keen eyesight and grasping tentacles. A rasping tooth-covered tongue and sharp beak quickly did away with prey.

Some scientists think *Tylosaurus* may have herded fish and other prey into shallow water for an easier attack. Dolphins and killer whales hunt this way today. Other scientists speculate that *Tylosaurus* was an ambush predator. Although it needed to surface for air, the giant reptile could lie on the sea bottom for several minutes until unsuspecting prey swam close enough to grab.

Like all mosasaurs, *Tylosaurus* was totally adapted to life in the sea. It never crawled on land. Scientists know that mosasaurs bore their young alive in the water. This was proven by the discovery of a mother mosasaur skeleton in South Dakota containing the fossils of young.

A smaller mosasaur species named *Clidastes* lived in the same nearshore habitat as *Tylosaurus*. *Clidastes* ate fish, squid, and ammonites. Ammonites were mollusks with beautiful spiral shells. They were related to squid and octopi and were common in all warm seas of the Cretaceous. The modern chambered nautilus is similar to the prehistoric ammonite.

Clidastes, Tylosaurus, and an ammonite were common predators in Cretaceous seas.

Judy Cutchins

One of the largest ammonites was *Placenticeras*. It had a shell as big around as a bicycle tire. Some of these shells have been discovered with mosasaur bite marks in them. The mosasaur would seize an ammonite, puncturing the shell with its front teeth. Then it would shake the shell until the soft-bodied animal inside was torn free and fell out.

Clidastes feasts on ammonites.

Dozens of piercing teeth line the jaws of *Clidastes*.

Dark puncture marks made by the teeth of *Clidastes* can be seen on this shell of a dinner plate–sized ammonite.

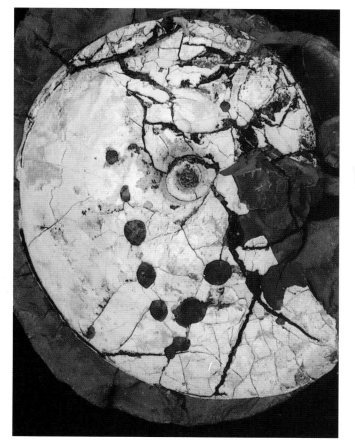

Clidastes vertebrae do not show large muscle attachment marks like those of *Tylosaurus*. Therefore, *Clidastes* was most likely not a long-distance swimmer or deep diver. It was a speedy hunter that chased its prey near the surface.

Mixed-up Fossils

When fossils of different kinds of animals are in the same rock layer at a dig site, scientists know the animals lived in the same habitat. Mollusks and other sea creatures found with mosasaur fossils are important clues about prehistoric ocean life.

One of the smallest mosasaurs ever discovered was found by an amateur fossil hunter in Alabama. The jaw of this baby *Clidastes* is just a few inches long.

A high school student looking for fossils near a small Alabama town uncovered pieces of a skeleton that turned out to be a rare discovery—a baby *Clidastes*. Scientists were so fascinated that they visited the site for several years, hoping to locate as many pieces of the small skeleton as possible. They were never able to find the entire animal because some fossils had been destroyed or washed away.

From the fossils found, scientists determined the baby's size and age. The bones of the small arm, or flipper, and other parts of the skeleton were not fully developed. Scientists estimated that the baby would have been only a few months old and just four feet long.

Mosasaurs lived throughout the Cretaceous in the warm seas of North America and Europe. Their fossils have also been discovered in Asia, Africa, South America, and New Zealand.

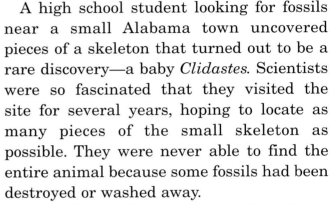

Undeveloped flipper bones helped scientists determine that the baby *Clidastes* was just a few months old.

This flipper of an adult *Clidastes* at the McWane Center in Birmingham, Alabama, shows complete bone development and is many times larger than the flipper of the baby.

Sizing Things Up

From certain bones, paleontologists can estimate the size of an animal. For example, for an adult *Clidastes* skeleton, they measure the length of the jaw and compare it to the length of the whole skeleton. This gives a jaw-to-body ratio. Measuring the jaw of the baby, they use the same ratio to estimate the length of the baby's skeleton.

fifteen jaw lengths

Ratio of jaw to body = 1:15

one jaw length

three

Strange Plesiosaurs

During the Cretaceous, mosasaurs were not the only giant reptiles in the seas. There were also enormous plesiosaurs. While whole skeletons have not been located in the South, paleontologists have found vertebrae, skull fragments, paddle bones, and teeth. Comparing these fossils to more complete skeletons from other states, scientists know that two groups of plesiosaurs swam in southern waters—elasmosaurs and pliosaurs.

Short-necked pliosaurs and long-necked elasmosaurs swam in the Cretaceous seas.

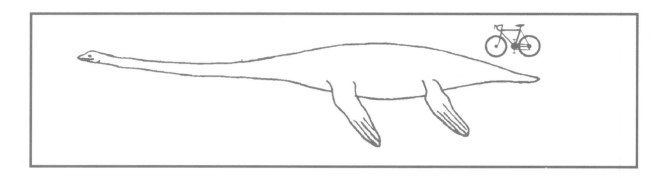

Elasmosaurs ate soft-bodied squid and small fish.
This skull is on display at the Tate Geological
Museum in Casper, Wyoming.

These 44 round stones, called gastroliths, were found inside the ribs of an elasmosaur. These stomach stones were swallowed by the animal.

Plesiosaurs with small heads and necks as long as their bodies are called elasmosaurs. At elasmosaur fossil sites, scientists have found dozens of smooth, rounded rocks alongside ribs. Many paleontologists think these stones, called gastroliths, were scooped up from the sea bottom and swallowed by the elasmosaurs to provide extra weight for staying underwater. Other scientists argue the stones helped grind and digest food. Stomach stones are still a plesiosaur mystery.

The fastest swimming plesiosaurs were the short-necked pliosaurs. They had wide tails and much larger heads than elasmosaurs. Swimming limbs, usually called paddles, were six feet long on some giant pliosaurs.

Teeth of plesiosaurs were sharp but slender. These sea reptiles could not have eaten large, bony prey because their teeth would have broken off. Instead, they feasted on soft-bodied squid and small fish. In order to catch such fast-moving targets, plesiosaurs had to be quick.

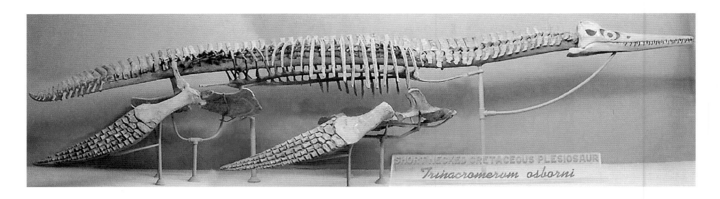

This skeleton of a plesiosaur can be seen at the Natural History Museum at the University of Kansas.

Flying Underwater

Sea turtles flap their flippers up and down in a flying motion underwater. Because the shape of a plesiosaur's paddle is much like that of a sea turtle's flipper, scientists think plesiosaurs swam the same way. By studying the shoulder joints, scientists know the plesiosaurs could also move their paddles back and forth to make quick turns.

Dozens of small bones make up this 3-foot-long pliosaur swimming paddle.

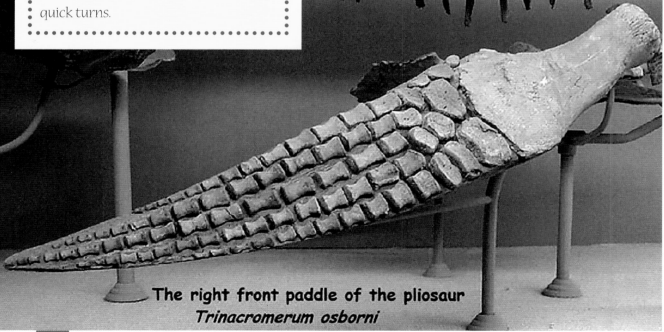

The right front paddle of the pliosaur
Trinacromerum osborni

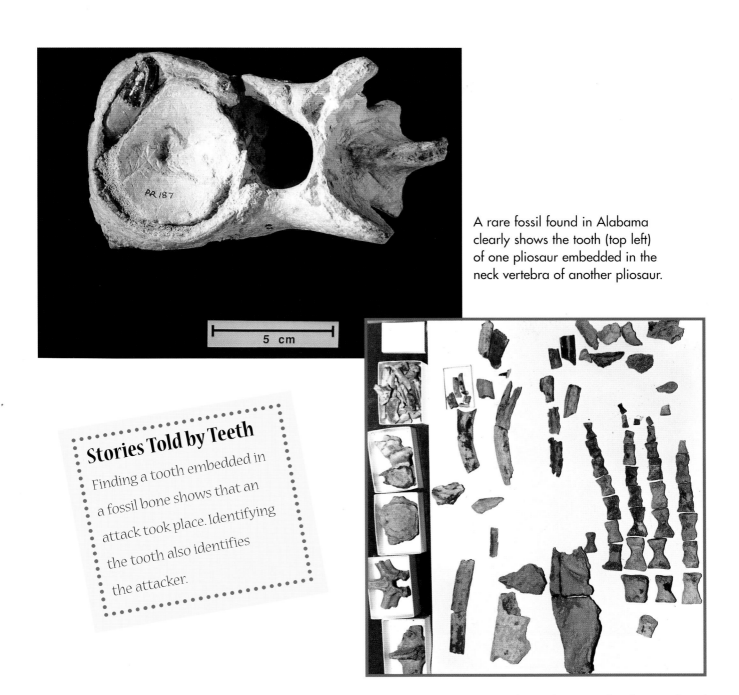

A rare fossil found in Alabama clearly shows the tooth (top left) of one pliosaur embedded in the neck vertebra of another pliosaur.

Stories Told by Teeth

Finding a tooth embedded in a fossil bone shows that an attack took place. Identifying the tooth also identifies the attacker.

These plesiosaur fossils were found at the same Alabama site as the vertebra above.

Although plesiosaurs did not hunt other plesiosaurs as food, there is evidence that they attacked each other. Plesiosaur teeth have been found embedded in the bones of other plesiosaurs. Maybe they fought to keep another animal from stealing their prey, to protect their young, or to defend their underwater territory.

Often, fossil skeletons of mosasaurs and plesiosaurs have vertebrae and limb bones missing. When these giant reptiles died, sharks and other scavengers fed on their bodies. Flippers and tails were easy for a scavenger to bite and tear away.

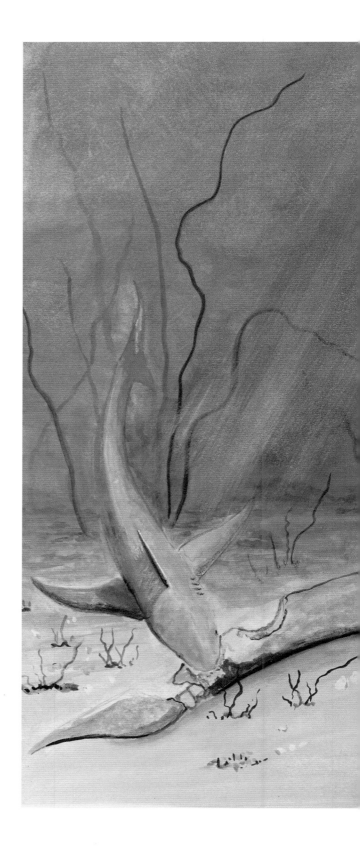

Cretaceous sharks found dead mosasaurs and plesiosaurs easy meals.

four

Awesome Fish

Several species of huge bony fish swam in the seas during the Cretaceous. One of the most frightening was *Xiphactinus,* or bulldog tarpon. This fierce predator had three-inch-long teeth protruding from awesome jaws. The bulldog tarpon was the biggest bony fish of the Cretaceous, reaching a length of eighteen feet and weighing over eight hundred pounds. Recently, vertebrae found in Arkansas have convinced paleontologists that even larger bulldog tarpon may have lived in the warm Cretaceous waters.

Although the prehistoric bulldog tarpon probably looked and behaved much like a modern tarpon, it was an ancient species not related to any modern fish. Fossils of the bulldog tarpon have been found in many parts of the world and in all North American states that were covered by the Cretaceous seas.

Bulldog tarpon

The fierce bulldog tarpon was the largest bony fish in the Cretaceous seas. This model skeleton is 12 1/2 feet long.

Xiphactinus audax
Sternberg Museum of Natural His

Another strange kind of fish that swam in the seas and rivers of prehistoric times was the coelacanth. There were many species of coelacanth, and some were truly giants. Fossils of a nine-foot-long species are known from sedimentary rocks dating back 140 million years. This awesome fish hunted near shore, where there was a variety of prey.

Until recently, paleontologists were sure all species of coelacanth went extinct about eighty million years ago. Then, in 1987, an amazing discovery was made in Alabama. Jaw bones and other fossils of a giant coelacanth were discovered in sedimentary rock layers that were just over sixty-five million years old. It was proof that there were still giant coelacanths swimming the seas at the end of the Cretaceous. The newly discovered species was larger than any ever discovered. The Alabama giant would have been eleven feet long. It was given the name *Megalocoelacanthus,* or huge coelacanth.

Since the identification of these fossils, more *Megalocoelacanthus* fossils have been located. Some fossils collected in Alabama and Georgia had been misidentified as dinosaur or mosasaur fossils. The large number of fossils found in recent years has led paleontologists to think the giant coelacanth was an important predator along the southern coasts. Even though it had no teeth, the giant coelacanth captured plenty of prey. Opening its gills and its mouth at the same time, the coelacanth would suck water, fish, and other animals inside like a powerful vacuum cleaner.

In 1952, this incredible fish-inside-a-fish fossil was found in Kansas. It shows a 6-foot-long prey inside the skeleton of a 14-foot bulldog tarpon.

Based on the fossils that have been found, scientists have been able to tell what a giant coelacanth looked like.

In 1938, fishermen in the Indian Ocean netted a live coelacanth. It was declared a "living fossil" although experts soon knew it was not the same species as those of the Cretaceous. The modern coelacanth is a deep-sea predator that grows up to six feet long and weighs one hundred pounds. Today's coelacanth may well be a living link to the ancient seas.

Sixty-five million years ago, the time of the giant fish and sea reptiles came to an abrupt end. Catastrophic events on earth brought about the extinction of these animals along with the extinction of dinosaurs and many other creatures. At the end of the Cretaceous, more than half of all the earth's species of plants and animals had disappeared forever.

The Cretaceous Extinction

There have been various theories about what caused so many species to go extinct at the end of the Cretaceous. Most scientists agree that a huge meteor struck the earth. Smoke, dust, and fire spread around the world and caused changes in climates. These changes were so sudden that many living things could not adapt and species died out.

These are spine, jaw, and fin fossils found at an Alabama dig site. Amazingly, these fragments were enough for paleontologists to estimate the size of an 11-foot-long coelacanth.

Real
Sea
Serpents

For millions of years after the Cretaceous, no fierce giant predators swam the seas. But in the early Eocene, a new era of giant sea predators was under way. Although the sea that once covered the middle of North America was replaced by dry land, much of the southern Coastal Plain remained underwater. The world's sea level was still higher than it is today. In those warm coastal waters of the South, a fearsome reptile lurked—an enormous sea snake scientists named *Pterosphenus*.

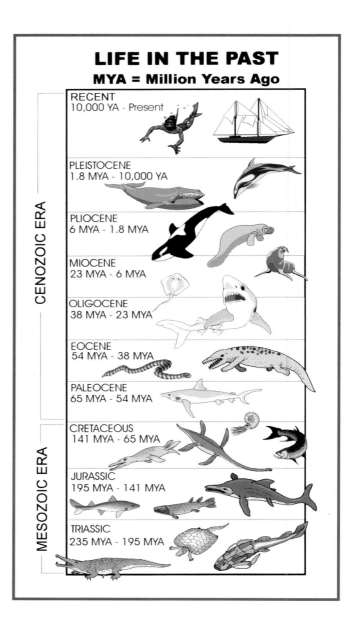

LIFE IN THE PAST

MYA = Million Years Ago

CENOZOIC ERA

RECENT
10,000 YA - Present

PLEISTOCENE
1.8 MYA - 10,000 YA

PLIOCENE
6 MYA - 1.8 MYA

MIOCENE
23 MYA - 6 MYA

OLIGOCENE
38 MYA - 23 MYA

EOCENE
54 MYA - 38 MYA

PALEOCENE
65 MYA - 54 MYA

MESOZOIC ERA

CRETACEOUS
141 MYA - 65 MYA

JURASSIC
195 MYA - 141 MYA

TRIASSIC
235 MYA - 195 MYA

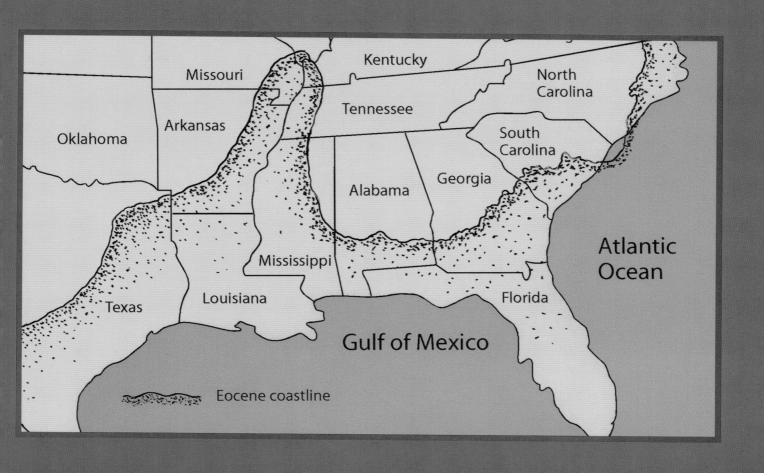

Missouri

Kentucky

North
Carolina

Oklahoma

Arkansas

Tennessee

South
Carolina

Alabama

Georgia

Atlantic
Ocean

Mississippi

Texas

Louisiana

Florida

Gulf of Mexico

Eocene coastline

Fossil vertebrae and ribs of *Pterosphenus* have been discovered in every southern coastal state. Along the eastern coast, fossils have been found as far north as New Jersey. *Pterosphenus* lived in other parts of the world too. Fossils have been identified in Ecuador and Egypt.

The largest land snake living today is the python. Although *Pterosphenus* matched the python in size, the shapes of the vertebrae and ribs were different from those of the python. They were more like those of sea snakes. *Pterosphenus* never ventured onto the shore. The Eocene snake's skeleton was not the right shape to support its estimated weight—seventy pounds—on land.

Pterosphenus lived in shallow coastal waters where rivers flow into the sea. These areas, where fresh water mixes with salt water, are called estuaries. Only certain

An 18-foot-long sea snake, *Pterosphenus*, inhabited warm coastal waters of the South during the Eocene.

kinds of animals can survive in estuaries. Tiger sharks, sand sharks, and stingrays are common in today's estuaries. Bones and teeth of prehistoric tiger sharks, sand sharks, and large rays, along with *Pterosphenus* fossils, have been found at Eocene fossil sites in Mississippi and Texas. These are important clues that prove these areas were estuaries more than thirty-eight million years ago.

Past and Present Sea Serpents

No entire skeleton of *Pterosphenus* has been found to prove its actual length. The size of *Pterosphenus* was estimated by comparing fossil vertebrae and ribs to those of a modern python nearly twenty feet long. Since the bones were a close match, scientists think the two snakes were about the same size.

This reticulated python living at the Hogle Zoo in Utah is 20 feet long and weighs 155 pounds.

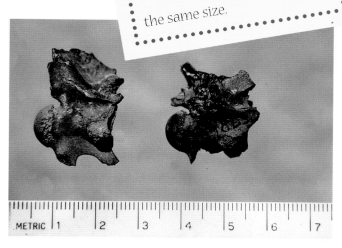

These fossil *Pterosphenus* vertebrae fragments were found at an Eocene site near Laredo, Texas.

41

One of the best Eocene locations in North America is near Laredo, Texas. Forty-two million years ago, the area was a large estuary bordered by dense tropical forests. At this location, fossils of twenty-nine extinct mammal species were found, along with fossils of crocodiles, turtles, sharks, rays, and giant sea snakes. Many fossilized shells of mollusks were also found.

Fossilized seeds, leaves, and pollen at the Texas site gave scientists more valuable information about this ancient coastal habitat. Some of the plant species have modern relatives that are found only in the tropics. Plants in these habitats need a great deal of rain and cannot survive winter freezes. This tells scientists that the Eocene climate in Texas, and therefore in the South, was much warmer and wetter than today.

During the Eocene, the coasts of southern North America looked much like this tropical forest in Costa Rica.

Students sort, clean, and record a variety of fossils found at a Texas location. The different plant and animal fossils help scientists develop an idea of what the prehistoric habitat was like.

Oysters live in calm waters that are exposed at low tide. Finding oyster shell fossils gives scientists important clues about the ancient shoreline environment.

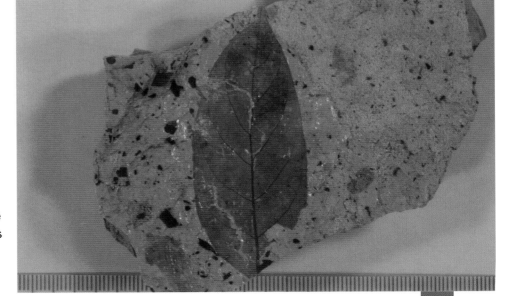

This fossil leaf print from a tropical hardwood tree is evidence that the Texas area was once a very warm habitat.

Six

First Toothed Whales

New kinds of sea predators swimming in the world's oceans during the Eocene included the first species of toothed whales. In the 1980s, fossils of a whale were uncovered by a construction crew in Georgia. Scientists from Georgia Southern University and Alabama's McWane Center were called in to recover the fossils. The whale was a species that lived forty-two million years ago and was the oldest whale ever found in North America. It was given the name *Georgiacetus*.

Scientists work carefully to chip rare whale fossils from limestone.

Naming Extinct Animals

Whenever fossils are discovered, scientists compare them to skeletons in paleontology collections for identification. If a new kind of animal is recognized, the discoverer gets to name it. He or she can invent the animal's scientific name, which is usually Latin or Greek.

This unusual whale had both front and back legs. It was a sea mammal that swam very well, but it could never leave the water. The back legs would not have supported the whale's enormous weight on land.

Enough fossils were found to give scientists an idea of what *Georgiacetus* might have looked like.

How Old Is That Fossil?

To determine the age of *Georgiacetus*, paleontologists used mollusk fossils found in the same rock. One was an oyster and another a small sea snail. Both lived from 40 to 42 million years ago and can be found only in sediments that formed at that time. Whale fossils found mixed with those mollusks would be the same age. Fossils that help scientists determine the age of rocks and other fossils are called index fossils.

Fossil teeth and a few bone fragments of what may be another *Georgiacetus* have been found in South Carolina. So far, there are not enough fossils for a positive identification.

The largest of all Eocene whales was *Basilosaurus*. Three times the size of a modern killer whale, this seventy-foot-long predator had jaws lined with piercing and slicing teeth. Fossils of a *Basilosaurus* were first found in Louisiana in the 1840s. Discoverers thought the fossils were from a huge sea reptile. They named their find *Basilosaurus*, which means "king of the lizards." Scientists studying more fossils determined *Basilosaurus* was not a reptile but a mammal. It was another very early species of whale.

How Big Was the Brain?

Although brains and other soft body parts decompose completely, scientists can determine how large an animal's brain was. They measure the space inside the skull where the brain would have been. Brain spaces of the Eocene whales were not very large compared to those of modern whales.

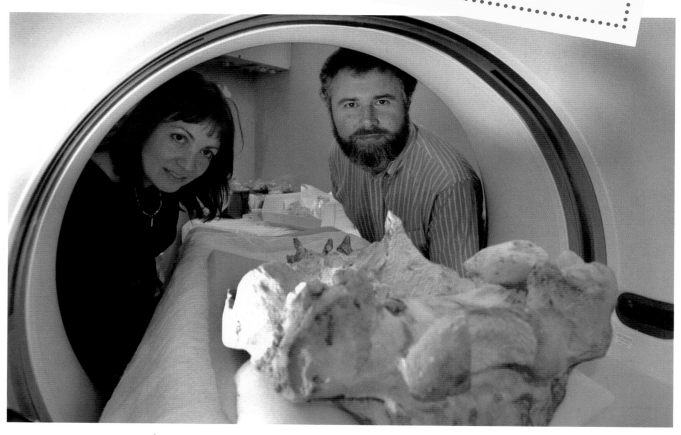

The skull of *Georgiacetus* was put through a CT scanner at Emory University in Atlanta to determine the size of the whale's brain space. CT scanners use a special X-ray technique to make pictures of bone.

The long, serpentlike body of the prehistoric whale
Basilosaurus caused discoverers to think it was a reptile.

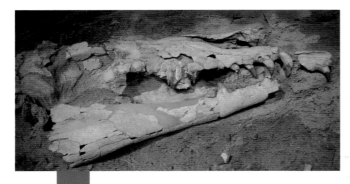

A *Basilosaurus* skull still partly buried in limestone is on
exhibit at the South Carolina State Museum in Columbia.
Large front teeth can be seen in the upper jaw.

Basilosaurus lived about forty million years ago. Although it had a tail like that of a modern whale, *Basilosaurus* was very different from any whale that lives now. Its extremely long body made it look more like a sea serpent than a whale. *Basilosaurus* had front flippers and tiny back legs that were of little use. This enormous predator was probably a good swimmer, but the shape of its skeleton convinced scientists it was not a deep diver.

Since the first *Basilosaurus* discovery in Louisiana, parts of skeletons have been found in Alabama, Mississippi, Florida, North and South Carolina, Georgia, Tennessee, and Arkansas. Scientists from all over the world visit these states to search for fossils of the first whales. *Basilosaurus* fossils have also been discovered in Great Britain and Egypt, proving this whale swam in many of the world's oceans.

In the early 1980s, an amateur fossil collector in Macon, Georgia, happened to uncover the skeleton of still another kind of Eocene whale, a *Zygorhiza*. Although it was smaller than *Basilosaurus*, the eighteen-foot-long *Zygorhiza* was a fearsome predator. The remains of its last meal were found in the stomach area. Not long before it died, *Zygorhiza* ate a two-foot-long shark. More *Zygorhiza* fossils have been found in the South than fossils of any other Eocene whale.

This impressive jaw fragment, with one enormous jagged tooth still in place, prompted legislators in Alabama to name *Basilosaurus* the state fossil.

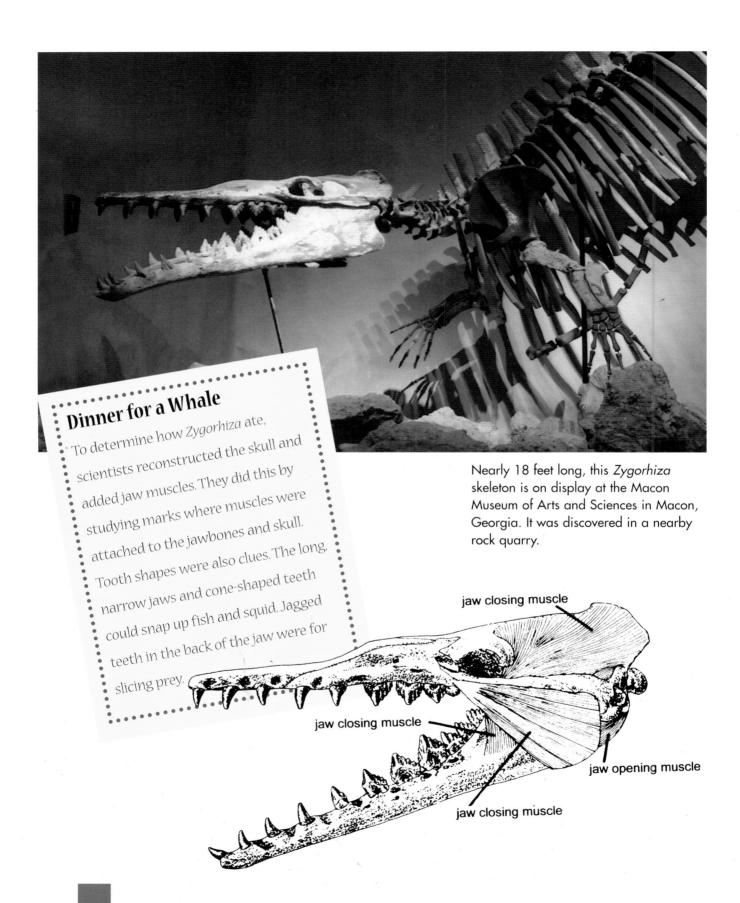

Dinner for a Whale

To determine how *Zygorhiza* ate, scientists reconstructed the skull and added jaw muscles. They did this by studying marks where muscles were attached to the jawbones and skull. Tooth shapes were also clues. The long, narrow jaws and cone-shaped teeth could snap up fish and squid. Jagged teeth in the back of the jaw were for slicing prey.

Nearly 18 feet long, this *Zygorhiza* skeleton is on display at the Macon Museum of Arts and Sciences in Macon, Georgia. It was discovered in a nearby rock quarry.

jaw closing muscle

jaw closing muscle

jaw opening muscle

jaw closing muscle

Scientists think all these Eocene whales went extinct by thirty-eight million years ago. No fossils of *Basilosaurus, Georgiacetus,* or *Zygorhiza* have ever been found in rock layers more recent than those of the Eocene.

As millions of years passed, a variety of new whale species appeared in southern waters. They became more adapted to life in the sea. Nostrils moved higher on their heads, and tails became wider and more powerful. In the southeastern United States, the best place to look for whales that lived during the Oligocene (thirty-eight to twenty-three million years ago) is the Coastal Plain of South Carolina. Since 1970, twenty-two new species of prehistoric whales have been discovered in South Carolina limestone. Most have not been named yet.

This 32-inch-long *Zygorhiza* skull is part of a skeleton at the Mississippi Museum of Natural Science in Jackson.

This whale lived 30 million years ago and is just one of the many whale fossils recently discovered in South Carolina.

Seven

Great Tooth Sharks

Among the largest sharks inhabiting southern seas during the Eocene were the first "great tooth" sharks. Their jaws were lined with hundreds of knife-sharp teeth. These sharks closely resembled modern great white sharks, but they were much larger. Some Eocene great tooth sharks reached forty feet, twice the length of a great white.

Judy Cutchins

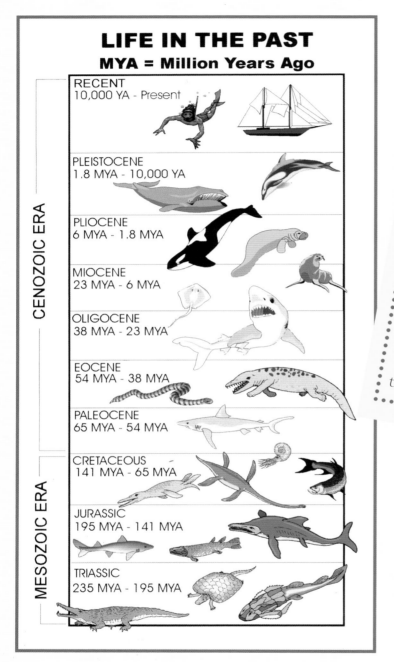

LIFE IN THE PAST
MYA = Million Years Ago

CENOZOIC ERA

RECENT
10,000 YA - Present

PLEISTOCENE
1.8 MYA - 10,000 YA

PLIOCENE
6 MYA - 1.8 MYA

MIOCENE
23 MYA - 6 MYA

OLIGOCENE
38 MYA - 23 MYA

EOCENE
54 MYA - 38 MYA

PALEOCENE
65 MYA - 54 MYA

MESOZOIC ERA

CRETACEOUS
141 MYA - 65 MYA

JURASSIC
195 MYA - 141 MYA

TRIASSIC
235 MYA - 195 MYA

Few Clues Left by Sharks

Most of a shark's skeleton is made of cartilage, which is softer than bone and often decomposes too quickly to fossilize. Only teeth and vertebrae are hard enough to become fossils.

By the time the Miocene began twenty-three million years ago, the earth's climate had cooled. Lower water temperatures caused changes in ocean life. During this time, the largest and most awesome species of great tooth shark ever to live appeared along the southern coast—*Carcharodon megalodon*. This fifty-foot-long monster thrived until just two million years ago.

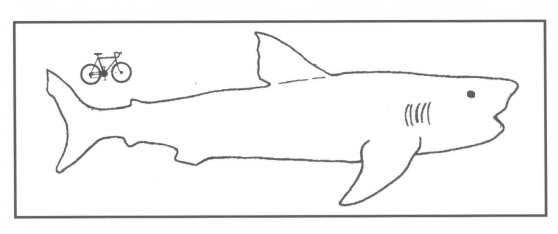

Measuring a Giant

The tooth of a large great white shark was compared to the shark's body length to get a tooth-to-body ratio. The tooth of *Carcharodon megalodon* was measured, and the same tooth-to-body ratio was used to estimate the animal's length. An adult *Carcharodon megalodon* was fifty feet long.

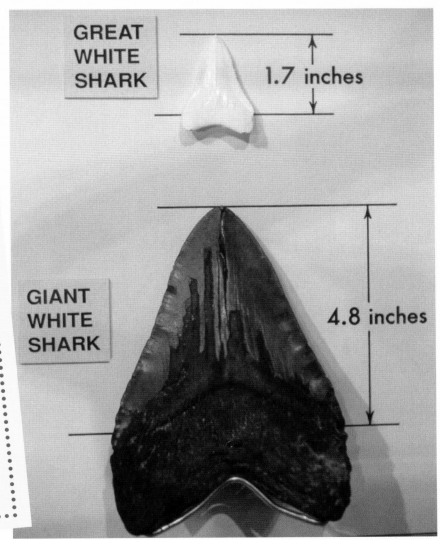

GREAT WHITE SHARK

1.7 inches

GIANT WHITE SHARK

4.8 inches

An adult *Carcharodon megalodon* weighed up to ten thousand pounds. Besides having very large teeth and jaws, the giant shark had a huge stomach and large intestines to process the animals it swallowed. For *Carcharodon megalodon* to be an efficient swimmer and predator, it would have had a wide tail and a very muscular body. Using this information, paleontologists recreated a life-size *Carcharodon megalodon* at the South Carolina State Museum.

Millions of Teeth

More shark teeth are found than any other kind of fossil. Scientists know there are not more sharks than any other animal, but each shark has many, many teeth. Shark teeth are not anchored in bony sockets, and they fall out easily. Losing teeth is not a problem because teeth are quickly replaced. A shark that lives ten years may lose thousands of teeth.

The giant among great tooth sharks was *Carcharodon megalodon*. This impressive 43-foot model amazes visitors at the South Carolina State Museum.

eight

Giant Sea Predators Today

There are still huge predators in the oceans. Great whites are the largest meat-eating sharks. At twenty feet, they are less than half the size of the extinct *Carcharodon megalodon*. Great white sharks hunt alone and cannot compete with killer whales. Killer whales grow larger than the great whites, up to twenty-five feet, and they hunt in very effective packs. Killer whales are nicknamed "sea wolves" because of their hunting behavior.

The largest sea predators today are sperm whales. These giants may reach more than sixty feet in length. Sperm whales are rarely seen near shore. They dive thousands of feet in search of giant squid and other deep-sea prey.

Life in the oceans has changed over time. Different species of predators have evolved to hunt new kinds of prey. Species of plants and animals have lived and gone extinct as long as there has been life on earth. Fossils from these earlier living things provide the only clues scientists have for understanding the past.

Unfortunately, many fossils that could provide valuable information about the past may remain hidden because the earth is constantly changing. For the last ten thousand years, the global climate has been gradually warming. With the rise in temperature, glaciers melt and cause a slow rise in sea level worldwide. More land where fossils might be found is being covered by water. Just as scientists know that change will always be a part of the earth's existence, they also know that many clues to the past will never be found.

Glossary

Carnivore—an animal that eats meat

Climate—general weather conditions in a region over a period of years

Cretaceous—geological time period from 65 to 141 million years ago

Eocene—geological time period from 38 to 54 million years ago

Fossil—the remains or traces of an organism preserved from past geologic ages

Limestone—a type of sedimentary rock formed primarily by shells of dead sea creatures

Miocene—geological time period from 6 to 23 million years ago

Mollusks—a group of soft-bodied animals, some of which are protected by a shell

Mosasaur—lizard of the Cretaceous that lived in the sea

Oligocene—geological time period from 23 to 38 million years ago

Paleontologist—a scientist who studies fossil evidence to interpret the past

Plesiosaur—Cretaceous sea reptile with large, oar-shaped paddles

Scavenger—an animal that feeds primarily on dead animals

Sediment—material that settles to the bottom in a body of water

Sedimentary rock—rock formed when layers of sediment are under tremendous pressure over long periods of time

Tarpon—type of saltwater fish

Tropical—referring to the warmest regions on earth

Vertebra (plural **vertebrae**)—part of an animal's spine, commonly called a backbone

Pronunciation Key

Ammonite	(AM uh nite)
Basilosaurus	(bas il uh SAWR us)
Carcharodon megalodon	(car CARE uh don) (MEG uh luh don)
Clidastes	(kly DAS tees)
Coelacanth	(SEE luh kanth)
Cretaceous	(kruh TAY shuhs)
Elasmosaurus	(ih LAZ muh SAWR us)
Eocene	(EE uh seen)
Georgiacetus	(JAWR juh SEET us)
Miocene	(MY uh seen)
Mosasaur	(MOH suh SAWR)
Oligocene	(oh LIG uh seen)
Placenticeras	(pluh SENT uh SER us)
Plesiosaur	(PLEE see uh SAWR)
Pliosaur	(PLY uh SAWR)
Pterygoids	(TER ih Go ids)
Pterosphenus	(TER us FEEN us)
Tylosaurus	(TY luh SAWR us)
Xiphactinus	(zy FAK tuh nus)
Zygorhiza	(ZY gor RIZE uh)

Index

Bold page numbers indicate illustrations.

If you enjoyed reading this book, here are some other books from Pineapple Press on related topics. Ask your local bookseller for our books. For a complete catalog, write to Pineapple Press, P.O. Box 3889, Sarasota, FL 34230 or call 1-800-PINEAPL (746-3275). Or visit our website at www.pineapplepress.com.

Southern **FOSSIL** discoveries ● vol. 1

Ice Age Giants of the South by Judy Cutchins and Ginny Johnston. First in the Southern Fossil Discoveries series, this book chronicles up-to-date discoveries in the field of archaeology and describes how prehistoric animals looked, how they lived, and what they ate. Includes full-color photos of fossil bones, reconstructed skeletons, and lifelike models of extinct creatures. ISBN 1-56164-195-2 (hb)

The Florida Water Story by Peggy Sias Lantz and Wendy A. Hale. Illustrates and describes many of the plants and animals that depend on the springs, rivers, beaches, marshes, and reefs in and around Florida, including corals, sharks, lobsters, alligators, manatees, birds, and turtles. ISBN 1-56164-099-9 (hb)

Florida's First People by Robin C. Brown. Filled with photos of replicas of technologies used by early peoples in their daily lives, this book brings to life the first humans who entered Florida about 12,000 years ago. Great for a budding archaeologist or historian! ISBN 1-56164-032-8 (hb)

Florida's Fossils by Robin Brown. Includes a complete identification section and insightful comments on the history of the fossil treasures you'll uncover. Amateur archaeologists will appreciate updated maps and directions to some of the best fossil-hunting areas in Florida. ISBN 1-56164-114-6 (pb)

The Young Naturalist's Guide to Florida by Peggy Sias Lantz and Wendy A. Hale. Plants, birds, insects, reptiles, and mammals are all around us. This enticing book shows you where and how to look for Florida's most interesting natural features and creatures. ISBN 1-56164-051-4 (pb)